The BIG BOOK of ICKS

Written by Tom Cullen, the creator of the Zoplo App
With contributions from Roseanna Leconte
First Published 2024

Contact tom.cullen@zoplo.co.uk for enquiries

Zoplo - Post. Vote. Debate.

Contents

Contents

Introduction: Icks through the ages

Ever since man first walked the earth, they have been giving women the ick.

Picture the scene: millions of years ago, an early form of the male homosapien returns from a day of hunting.

The female anticipates his arrival with excitement for a hearty meal provided by her courageous partner.

He returns to unveil the glorious meal: two floppy fish from the nearby river.

This was not the feast she was promised. She grunts at him. She wonders why she ever chose this man.

She's got the ick.

Fast forward a few ice ages, and we are now in ancient Egypt in 3000BC.

A man, dressed fit for a pharaoh, is making an attempt to charm the most beautiful woman in the village.

He's flirting, she's blushing, it's all going far too well.

He's wearing a headdress to display his wealth, in the hopes of wooing this woman.

He takes a step towards her, the headdress falls off.

She takes a step back.

She's got the ick.

A few more centuries later, we are in Victorian England.

An upper-class gentleman writes a love letter to his mistress and sends it her way with a pigeon.

The pigeon drops off the wax-sealed letter at her window, and she falls onto her bed overcome with love and flattery.

She opens the letter.

She can't read his ghastly handwriting.

You see where this is going.

She's got the ick.

Today, many millennia later, we have been blessed with the vocabulary to define this feeling of repulsion.

Whilst men may no longer be hunting for meat, they have never ceased in their unmatched ability to give women everywhere the infamous ick.

The digital age brought with it a new myriad of ways that men can prove how icky they really are.

Our trusty friend, the Oxford English Dictionary, dates the term ick back to the 1940s to describe people who did not appreciate true swinging jazz music.

It wasn't until the 1980s that the ick factor gained popularity for its use in describing something as repulsive, and a decade longer before it applied specifically to romantic turn-offs.

For educational purposes only, we recommend watching Season 1, Episode 22 of *Friends*: 'The One with the Ick Factor'.

In the 21st century, the newfound popularity of the term has often been attributed to Olivia Atwood on the third series of Love Island in 2017.

Six years later, songs about the ick are getting millions of streams on Spotify, and there is an entire side of TikTok dedicated to it – IckTok (@zoplohalloffame for the best icks out there).

We all know the classics – bad body odour, eating with their mouth open, and being rude to a waiter.

But with a new generation of dating, particularly amongst Gen Z, the icks are now more niche than ever.

It has never been easier for men to know exactly what puts off potential girlfriends, thanks to a handy checklist of what not to do.

And now, in 2024, thousands of icks have been posted and voted on in the Zoplo app.

In this book we showcase some of the cringiest, skin crawling, vomit inducing icks out there.

Next to every ick there is an 'ick score'.

This is the percentage of people that thought it was an ick. The number of votes below is how many people voted in the 'ick or stick' poll.

All votes have been cast in the Zoplo app.

So grab a friend, put the kettle on, and prepare to get the ick.

EWWW

I'VE GOT THE ICK

Ick score:
The percentage of people that think it is an ick. They voted for 'ick' in the Zoplo poll rather than voting for 'stick'. The higher the percentage, the more people thought is was an ick e.g. a 60% ick score mean that 60% of people that voted in the poll think it is an ick.

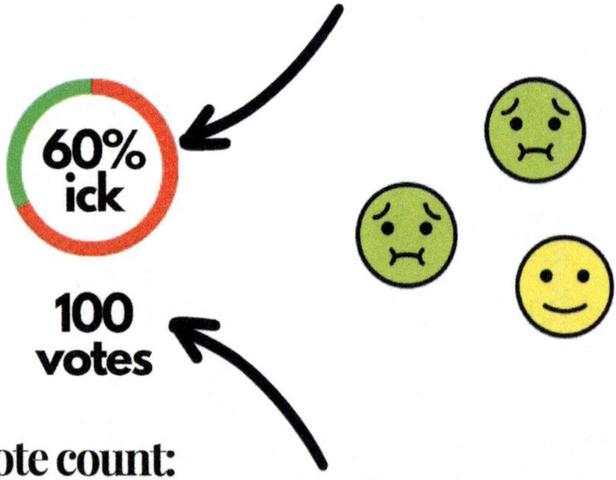

Vote count:
The number of people that voted in the Zoplo poll on whether the behaviour is an 'ick' or a 'stick' e.g. 100 votes means 100 people in total voted in the poll. 60 of those think it was an 'ick', whilst 40 thought it was a 'stick'.

Part 1:
Awkwaaardd

67% ick

82 votes

When the barber spins him around for **the grand reveal**

BONUS ICK

The chair **swivels too much** and he spins around twice

YOU SPIN ME RIGHT ROUND BABY, RIGHT ROUND

LIKE A BARBER SHOP REVEAL BABY, RIGHT ROUND

132 votes

When you ask him a question and he replies in a **weird cartoon voice**

THE ICK
HE HAS GIVEN ME

78
votes

When he says he knows the bouncer at the club and they have **no idea who he is**

BONUS ICK

He goes to shake their hand and they **blank him**

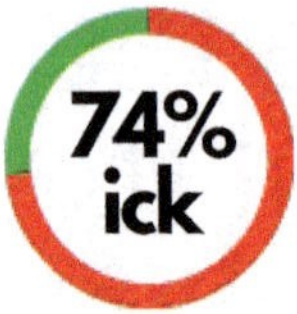

80
votes

When he's **always hugging** and kissing his sister on the forehead

BONUS ICK

He **holds hands** with her in public

138 votes

When he doesn't know the lyrics so **mumbles made up words** hoping people don't notice

BONUS ICK

The **music stops** and everyone looks at it

195
votes

Imagine him stood in a fast food joint with a **tray full of food** and there is nowhere to sit

BONUS ICK

He's bought a **fish based** burger

238 votes

When he messages you after the date: "What would you have done if I **kissed you**?"

HUN

I WOULD HAVE THROWN UP

297 votes

Imagine him sat on a sofa at a party, people either side are having a conversation, he tries to join in and **they ignore him**

BONUS ICK

He **pretends** to be on his phone

1,820 votes

When he says a joke in a group, **nobody laughs** so he then explains his joke

BONUS ICK

It was a joke involving **toilet humour**

Part 2:
He might as well have two left feet

258 votes

When he chases a **ping pong ball** and can't catch it

142 votes

When he does his shoe laces really tight so they have that **massive bow**

**309
votes**

Imagine you're at a **water park** and he's waiting for the lifeguard to tell him to go down the slide

BONUS ICK

The life guard is deliberately **ignoring** him

Please can I go Mr. lifeguard?

182
votes

When the automatic door **doesn't open** so he walks back and forth

BONUS ICK

He **thanks the door** when it finally opens

142 votes

Imagine him walking into the sea, he **steps on a pebble** and loses his balance

158 votes

When he sleeps hugging his **pillow**

216 votes

When he climbs down from the top bunk and his **feet are dangling** trying to find the ladder

BONUS ICK

He has **holes in his socks** and his big toe sticks out

227 votes

When he's trying to stand up on a paddleboard but **can't balance** so falls off it

BONUS ICK

He swims after the paddleboard but **can't catch it**

Noooooo!!!!
I'm going down!

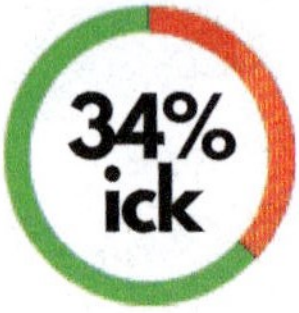

191
votes

Imagining him **hunched over** trying to balance a plate of food on his knees

BONUS ICK

He **drops his plate** and peas fall all over the floor

325 votes

Imagine you get in an argument and he **hits himself** in the head repeatedly because he's upset

BONUS ICK

A **lump appears** on his forehead afterwards

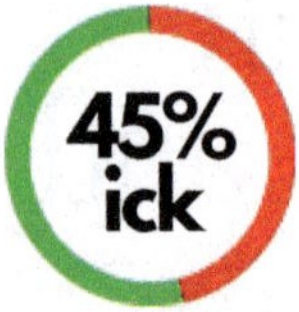

310 votes

When he can't get control of his **umbrella** in the wind

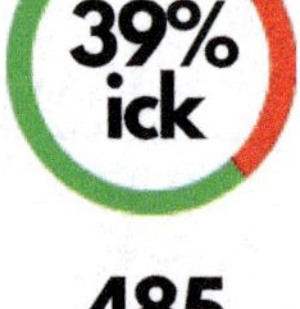

485 votes

When he wakes up really confused and screams "**urrrrr**" before looking around to work out where he is

It's just a light gust of wind

31% ick

278 votes

Imagine him trying to **crack an egg** in a little egg cup with a teaspoon and the shell won't break

BONUS ICK

He's **singing humpty dumpty** whilst he does it

1,086 votes

Imagine him running up the stairs **on all fours**

BONUS ICK

You chase him up and **he farts** in your face

1,000 votes

When he **trips over** loose pavement and does that weird little fall

BONUS ICK

His **arms are flailing** in the air as he goes down

4,682 votes

Imagine going for a morning walk and he gets one of those **snot bubbles** forming under his nose

BONUS ICK

He tries to **kiss you** with snot on his face

1,182
votes

When he steps onto the road to cross but a car comes so he does the **little hop back** on to the pavement

BONUS ICK

He gets **hit by a car**

2,294 votes

When he takes **mirror selfies**

BONUS ICK

He says "**Phwoaarrr**" whilst doing it

Phwoooaarrr!!!

575 votes

Imagine him falling asleep with his mouth open and a bit of **drool running down** his chin

BONUS ICK

He doesn't wipe it off and goes to work with it **still on his chin**

31% ick

461 votes

You swing him around during "**cotton eyed joe**" so hard he crashes into loads of tables

BONUS ICK

He runs off crying screaming **"I need an adult!!"**

378
votes

Imagine him trying to get involved in a **mosh pit** and getting bullied out of the circle straight away

BONUS ICK

He's doing the **rock symbol** with his hands as he hits the ground

236
votes

Imagine him trying to ride a **mechanical bull** as he gets thrown from side to side

BONUS ICK

He's screaming "Yeee-Hawww"

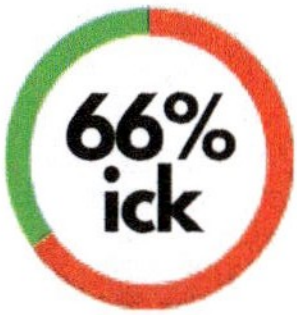

280 votes

He comes over to ask you out, gets nervous, **veins start appearing** on his head like he's trying to hold in a fart

BONUS ICK

He farts and **sh*ts himself**

Part 3: It’s not quirky, it’s an ick

80 votes

When he turns his pen into a drumstick and **makes a beat** before looking at you and laughing

BONUS ICK

He does it **every 30 minutes** to annoy you

45% ick

40 votes

When he goes out in a **nightgown holding a candle** saying "who goes there?"

BONUS ICK

He's wearing slippers and a **night hat**

Who goes there?

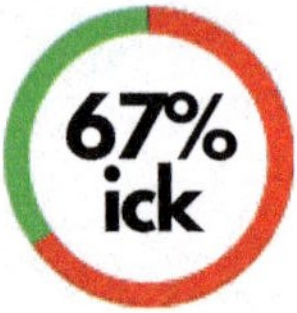

42 votes

When he approaches you saying "Well **moisten my meat**, aren't you looking sweet"

119 votes

When he says: "**omg lanaaaa**" in reference to Lana Del Rey

128 votes

When he uses the phrase "**Jiminy Christmas**"

"JEE-WIZZ JIMINY CHRISTMAS"

155 votes

When you go on holiday and he puts on **swimming goggles** in the pool

BONUS ICK

He needs **armbands**

140 votes

When his hat blows off in the wind and he **chases** after it

176 votes

When he starts a **Mexican wave** and nobody joins in

53%
ick

168
votes

When he gets cold, looks at you, does that **strange little shiver**, then says

"BRRRRR SHIVER ME TIMBERS"

Brrrrr!! Shiver me timbers

376 votes

When you're **doing the deed** and he says "oh my gooodness" over and over again

"OHHHH MY GOODNESS"

221 votes

He comes into your bedroom in the morning saying: "**wakey wakey** eggs and bakey"

BONUS ICK

He cooks the bacon in the **oven**

239 votes

He always **speaks to strangers** when you go out together

406 votes

His best friend is somebody of the **opposite sex**

328
votes

Imagine him using the phrase "**fiddle-de-dee**" in everyday life

"I GOT FIRED FROM WORK, FIDDLE-DE-DEE"

334 votes

Imagine him **playing the flute** whilst hopping side to side from one leg to the other

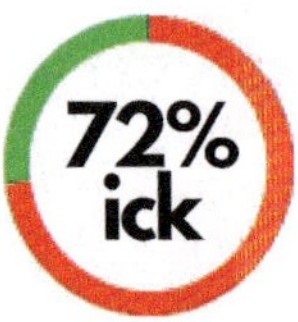

1,683 votes

Imagine him saying phrases like "**yoinks**" or "**jeepers**"

525 votes

Imagine him sending you an audio message and it's him **singing you a song**

BONUS ICK

He keeps getting the **words wrong**

942 votes

Imagine him singing **a cappella** to you with his eyes closed

BONUS ICK

He's making loads of **facial expressions**, a vein appears on his head

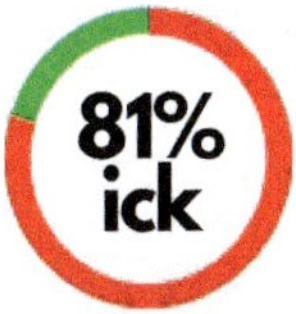

1,643 votes

Imagine him holding one finger in the air as he **corrects you** on your grammar

HUN,

I'M NOT LOOKING TO DATE A DICTIONARY

1,531 votes

He can't figure out which way the arrow is pointing on maps so **spins around** in a circle trying work it out

"GRRRRR WHICH WAY DO WE GO?!"

Part 4: Just when you thought it couldn't get any worse

89 votes

When he refers to girls as "**birds**"

82 votes

When he's **elitist** about the university somebody went to

36
votes

When he does a 4 **hour shift** at work, that's not a proper shift

BONUS ICK

He gets paid **below minimum wage** too

Babe that shift has destroyed me

151
votes

When he sits on a stool and his **legs dangle** down. It looks like he's in a highchair

BONUS ICK

You look and he's wearing **light up trainers**

153
votes

When they use the word "**moist**"

"HEY BABE DO YOU GET MOIST WHEN I TALK DIRTY TO YOU?"

110
votes

Imagine him having to use one of the long **metal rods** to get something from the top shelf

176
votes

When he has a **tribal tattoo** on his arm

471
votes

Imagine finding out his middle name is **Keith**

BONUS ICK

He wants to **call your first born** Keith.... even if it's a girl

4,050 votes

Imagine him owning a **pitbull called sprinkles**

BONUS ICK

He **can't control sprinkles** when he takes him on walks

48%
ick

629
votes

When he always says "**brought**" instead of "**bought**"

"HEY BABE I BROUGHT A MEMBERSHIP TO THE LOCAL GYM"

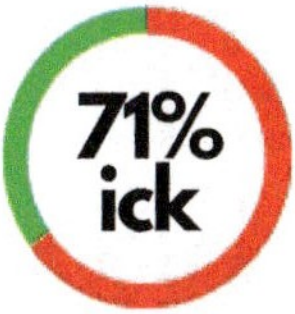

2,449 votes

When he calls women **females**

1,879 votes

When he says **"I'm not like other guys"**

1,636 votes

When he has a **Sigma male** quote as his phone background

"A MAN'S FINEST COLOGNE IS THE SWEAT FROM HIS GRIND"

Part 5:
His online presence is a bigger ick

65 votes

When he is way too involved in **online debates** with strangers

BONUS ICK

He cries when he **loses the debate**

73
votes

He's bottom of his **fantasy football league**

BONUS ICK

He supports a team from a country he's **never been to**

1,162 votes

When he's 29 but spends his weekends **dressed as an elf** pretending to fight other men

BONUS ICK

The font on his phone is Comic Sans

284 votes

When he wants to **message constantly**

"BABE...

HAVE I DONE SOMETHING WRONG? HAVEN'T HEARD FROM YOU IN THE LAST HOUR"

**281
votes**

Imagine him **hitting his games controller** against the sofa out of anger

BONUS ICK

A **vein appears** on his forehead

286 votes

Imagine him accusing somebody of **stealing his hammer** on an online video game

"HEY MAN,

I KNOW IT WAS YOU THAT STOLE MY HAMMER, I WANT IT BACK!!"

315 votes

Imagine him going up to a sorting hat and getting hufflepuff

PLS DON'T SUE US

BONUS ICK

He pronounces it **leviosaaa not leviosa**

99 votes

Imagine him bragging about how good at fifa he is and then you **beat him 3 - 0**

PLS DON'T SUE US

BONUS ICK

You are **Wigan**, he is **Liverpool**

Part 6:
Proof he needs to grow up

99 votes

He finds **toilet humour** funny and sends fart jokes in his lads group chat

BONUS ICK

Nobody replies to him

49 votes

He still sleeps with a **teddy**

BONUS ICK

He's making weird noises when he snores "**honk-shoo**"

Honk Shoo
Honk Shoo

141 votes

Imagine him being 29 and he still does **magic tricks**

BONUS ICK

He guessed the 8 of spades but it was the **7 of diamonds**

136 votes

When he screams "wooooooo!" on a **roller coaster**

BONUS ICK

His **arms are flailing about** in the air

170
votes

When he calls the deed **"Shnuggles"**

"HEY BABE, IT'S SHNUGGLE TIME"

213 votes

When he calls his mum **mummy**

BONUS ICK

He also **calls you mummy**

43%
ick

520
votes

Imagine him in a **potato sack race**

BONUS ICK

He **trips over** and smacks his face on the ground

3,147 votes

Imagine him playing **crack the egg** on a trampoline and he's the egg

1,736 votes

When he says "**nawww**"

662 votes

Imagine him getting a paper cut then coming up to you saying he has a 'boo boo' and **needs a plaster**

436 votes

He holds his hand to his mouth and does a little "**tehehe**"

2,578 votes

Imagine him asking you out on a date in person, you say yes and then he starts doing the **floss dance** to celebrate

BONUS ICK

A **vein appears** on his forehead

3,950 votes

He asks you out in person. You say yes. He walks off, jumps and **clicks his heels** in the air

BONUS ICK

On landing he **falls over**

77%
ick

274
votes

He **lets out a fart**, laughs, and then proceeds to sing

"BEANS BEANS

THE MAGICAL FRUIT, THE MORE YOU EAT, THE MORE YOU TOOT"

Part 7:
It's giving weird vibez

231 votes

When he has **no lamps** in their bedroom and just uses the main light

BONUS ICK

He **hisses at you** like a cat when you try to switch it off

134 votes

He texts you "good morning beautiful" **every morning**

BONUS ICK

Even after you **blanked** his "good night beautiful" text

181
votes

When you say "hahaha" and he replies with **"what's funny?"**

NOT YOU
HUN

175
votes

When he **smiles at everything** for no reason

HUN,

I'VE JUST TOLD YOU MY NAN DIED

2,191 votes

When he's **overly politically correct** and always corrects you

"BABE,

THAT MAN ISN'T BALD, HE'S FOLLICLY CHALLENGED"

1,448 votes

When you go for dinner and **he complains** that he could have cooked the food at home and saved money

BONUS ICK

He's a sh*t cook

Part 8:
He's ruined mealtimes

101 votes

When he **wiggles his fingers** as he goes for some food and says: "don't mind if I do"

BONUS ICK

He takes it **from your plate**

71%
ick

85
votes

When he has a piece of food **in his teeth** and it just won't come out

BONUS ICK

He tries to get it out with a **tiny toothpick**

147 votes

When he slurps his soup and makes the "**ahhhh**" noise afterwards

BONUS ICK

His go–to soup is **onion soup**

54 votes

When he posts a **boomerang** drinking cheap cocktails

BONUS ICK

His phone camera is grainy and **blurry**

129
votes

When he tests ice cream with one of those **baby tester spoons**

BONUS ICK

He doesn't know where to put it **afterwards**

231
votes

When he eats something hot and repeats "**owf owf owf**"

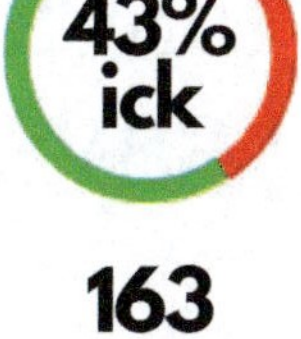

163
votes

When he doesn't finish his food so asks for a **doggy bag** to take it home

245
votes

Imagine him climbing into a restaurant booth on **all 4s**

BONUS ICK

He looks at you, **raises his eyebrows** and says "hop in"

218 votes

Whenever you go out for food they **ask the waiter** what to order and then blindly order it

166 votes

When he **leaves his crusts**

365 votes

Imagine him drinking **milk straight from the carton**

BONUS ICK

He has a **milk moustache** afterwards

546
votes

He chooses a **hard boiled egg** as his meal deal snack item

BONUS ICK

He picks it up and eats it with his **hands**

470 votes

When he washes his hands in a little **finger bowl** at a restaurant

2,074 votes

When he orders a **tuna and pineapple** pizza

1,941 votes

Imagine him eating spaghetti and having **orange sauce stains** around his mouth

507 votes

Imagine him **nibbling** on his chicken wings like a hamster

955 votes

Imagine him **shouting at a waiter** over how the food was cooked

"HOW DARE U
I WILL NOT BE
LEAVING A TIP!!"

Part 9:
My dad knows more about fashion

279 votes

Imagine him showing up for a date wearing **dirty white trainers**

BONUS ICK

With his laces tied in **huge bows**

61% ick

803 votes

Imagine him wearing a suit jacket that's too big and the **sleeves come past his hands**

BONUS ICK

It's his **dads...**

1,082 votes

Imagine him turning up to your house with a **backpack**

BONUS ICK

Imagine him **running for a bus** wearing it

Part 10:
Beep beep!

357 votes

Imagine him riding a bike with a **basket on the front**

BONUS ICK

He rings the **little bell**

89
votes

When he gets caught in the **train doors**

BONUS ICK

Or worse, he runs for the train and **misses it**

1,054
votes

Imagine his **earlobes blowing manically** on a windy boat

BONUS ICK

He's wearing an **oversized life jacket**

68% ick

53 votes

He says he drives and then comes to pick you up 'driving' an **electric bike**

"VROOM VROOM"

50%
ick

114
votes

When he pulls up in his **tiny car** to pick you up and says:

"BEEP BEEP
ALL ABOARD"

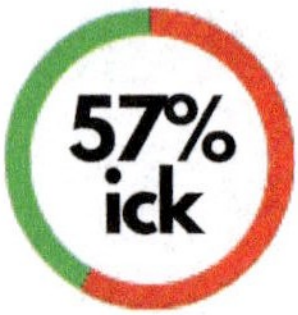

182
votes

Imagine him **sprinting down the train platform** waving bye as your train pulls off

BONUS ICK

He **trips over** halfway down the platform

1,936 votes

Imagine him learning to drive with a **big L** on the car

375 votes

Imagine him **scooting around** on a Vespa, beeping at traffic

1,816 votes

Imagine him riding past you on a **scooter** shouting as he goes by

"NEEOOOOMM

NEEOOOOMM"

55 votes

He posts pictures of him **stood posing** in front of a car

BONUS ICK

It's not even his **car**

Part 11:
I can't get merry with him around

51
votes

He says "babe let's **kiss under the mistletoe**", but when he goes to hang it up his arms are too short to reach

BONUS ICK

He gets out a **step ladder**

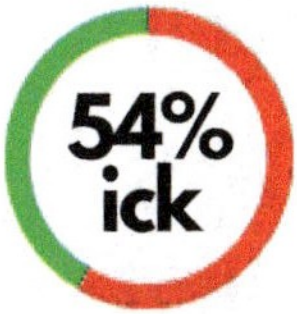

2,063 votes

Imagine him **hitting himself** in the head because he can't untangle the fairy lights

BONUS ICK

It turns out they're **not even tangled**

340 votes

He pulls the **Christmas cracker** but can't snap it

"GRRRRR THIS CARDBOARD IS TOO STRONG"

641 votes

He storms off in a **strop** because he doesn't get what he wanted for Christmas

HE'S 29

54%
ick

666
votes

You come downstairs and catch him **dressed as an elf**, hopping from side to side shouting

"6 MORE DAYS UNTIL SANTA COMES"

549 votes

Imagine you wearing a matching **Christmas pajama** set

BONUS ICK

He calls them his **crimbo jammies**

17% ick

326 votes

When he uses the **chocolate box menu** to pick a chocolate

BONUS ICK

He picks one he doesn’t like and has to **spit it out**

770
votes

He has **ketchup** with his Christmas dinner

BONUS ICK

He has **gravy too** and they mix together

313
votes

Imagine finding out he was a **made up side character** in his school nativity

ALIEN

LOBSTER

TREE

SHEEP

Part 12:
Personal hygiene 101

47
votes

He **doesn't cut his fingernails** and they scratch you when you hold hands

BONUS ICK

He **screeches** like a pterodactyl when you tell him he scratched you

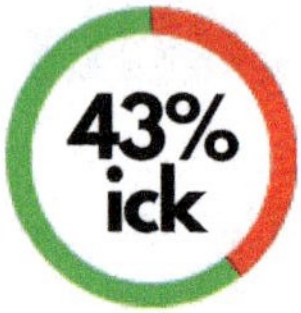

317 votes

Imagine him running from the shower to his bedroom on his **tip toes**

BONUS ICK

He's only covered by one of those **small towels**

398
votes

Imagine laying in bed with him and his **long toenails cut you**

BONUS ICK

He's taking up **90% of the bed** as well

534 votes

When he has one really **long nose hair** sticking out

BONUS ICK

He refuses to **cut** it

473
votes

When he calls the toilet the "**little boys room**"

"I NEED
A PEE PEE"

912 votes

Imagine him **sitting on the toilet**

BONUS ICK

He’s reading a broadsheet **newspaper**

1,494 votes

He puts water in **2-in-1** body wash & shampoo to make it "last longer"

HUN,

THAT'S NOT THE ONLY THING THAT NEEDS TO LAST LONGER

183
votes

Imagine him having a bubble bath and he gives himself a **bubble beard**

BONUS ICK

He drinks wine in the bath with his **pinky stuck out**

Fin.

Zoplo is a brand new social app where you can vote in everything from what gives you the ick, to hot topics and funny questions.

Contact tom.cullen@zoplo.co.uk for any enquiries.

Printed in Great Britain
by Amazon

37528967R00096